PETS

Dogs 2
Cats 6
Rabbits and Rodents 10
Tortoises and Terrapins 16
Fish 18
Birds 22

Kingfisher Books

Dogs

Dogs were first kept by people thousands of years ago. To begin with they were used for hunting, and they probably all looked much the same. But as they began to be used for different kinds of work, so different breeds were developed to do different jobs. Some dogs still work for a living today, such as the lively black-and-white Border Collie, which still herds sheep in many parts of the world.

However, most dogs are now just kept as pets. They come in many shapes and sizes, and their characters can also be very different. All types need a lot of care and attention, and it is very unfair to keep a dog unless you are prepared to give it plenty of exercise and company. Dogs also love to be trained, and you will find that an obedient pet is far more fun to own than a badly-behaved one.

Dalmation The spots of the Dalmation make it an easy breed to recognize. The smooth coat is always white, with spots of black or brown. It is an energetic and good-natured dog, and was probably once kept for hunting. It still likes to lead an active life, and needs plenty of exercise.

Rough Collie This handsome dog was first bred in Scotland as a work animal. Today it is bred for the showroom rather than for work. Its kindly face and sweet nature also make it a favourite pet. It has a long, rough coat, usually in brown and white.

Border Collie The hard-working Border Collie is one of the best sheepdogs in the world, and has been used on farms for hundreds of years. It is usually black and white, with short hair on the face and legs and longer hair on the body. It may be too lively to keep as a pet.

Welsh Springer Spaniel This is a hunting dog, well-known for its willingness to work even in bad weather conditions and on rough ground. It has a strong, sturdy body, with a silky coat of pearly white with reddish markings. Its floppy ears hang close to the cheek.

St Bernard This large dog has a gentle, kindly look. It was once used by monks in the Swiss Alps to carry supplies and act as a guide and rescuer in the mountain snow. Its thick, rough coat is white and golden brown, with black markings on the face. A grown St Bernard is a very large dog indeed, and one that needs plenty of space.

Corgi Corgis are active and noisy little dogs. They are traditionally used for herding cattle, but have also become well-known as the favourite pets of the British Royal Family. The Cardigan Corgi has a long furred tail, but this is cut to a short stump in the Pembroke.

5

Cats

A well-fed cat curled up on a sunny windowsill, or purring gently on its owner's lap, is a picture of homeliness and contentment. But this favourite family pet is also a relation of the lion and the tiger. At the first sign of a mouse or a bird, it uncurls itself and springs into action. Suddenly it is a skilful hunter, stalking its prey with stealth and cunning.

These fascinating animals were once thought to have strange, unearthly powers. The early Egyptians worshipped cats as gods, and held feasts in their honour. Cats living in the Middle Ages in Europe were less fortunate. The superstitious people living at this time thought they helped witches to cast their spells, and sadly many cats were put to their death.

Today, the cat is one of our best-loved pets. It enjoys human company and can be very affectionate, but is still fairly easy and cheap to care for.

British Short-hair, Bi-coloured British Short-haired cats are strong and short-legged, with a rounded head and small ears set well apart. The eyes are large, widely spaced, and often bright copper or orange. Cats of this type come in many colours and markings. The Bi-coloured has a coat patched with white and one other colour. The second colour may be black, red, blue or cream.

British Short-hair, Standard Tabby The Standard Tabby, with its coat of blotches, stripes and whorls, is a very popular pet. Standard Tabby cats can be different colours, but the markings are much the same. There is also a breed known as the Mackerel Tabby, where the stripes are narrower and more tiger-like.

Foreign Short-hair, Siamese The slinky-looking Siamese is an affectionate, intelligent cat which can be trained to wear a collar and lead. It has a long body, with slim legs and dainty oval paws.

Persian These long-haired cats have strong, heavy bodies with sturdy legs, large round paws and broad heads. The tail is very fluffy, and there is a ruff of fur on the neck and chest. Persian cats must be groomed often, to stop the fur getting tangled. Like short-hairs, they can come in many different colours and markings.

Rabbits and Rodents

Rabbits and rodents are gnawing animals, with strong front teeth that keep growing all their lives.

Rabbits have been known in Europe for hundreds of years, but until quite recently they were only kept for their fur and meat. They are now very popular pets, with about 35 breeds to choose from. Guinea pigs were first brought to Europe from South America in the 16th century. In the wild, they make their homes in tunnels trodden through the grass. Hamsters are burrowing animals from the deserts of Syria. To avoid the hot sun, they sleep by day and come out at night to feed. As pets, they are still more lively by night than by day. Tame mice and rats are now popular pets, and will happily live in cages, but rats and mice should never be mixed in the same cage.

English Fancy Breed Rabbit
This is a very popular breed of rabbit. The main colour is white, with markings of a second colour. Black and white are very common. It should have a dark line along the spine, dark ears, nose and eyes with spots along its sides. It is quite large, weighing about 4 kilograms.

Netherland Dwarf Rabbit
These are the smallest breed of rabbits, sometimes weighing only 1 kilogram. They make good pets, as they have a gentle nature and are easy to handle. The coat can be single-coloured or patterned.

Rough-haired Abyssinian Guinea Pig Some pet guinea pigs look quite different from their short-haired cousins which live in the wild. The Abyssinian has been specially developed to have a rough coat, which sticks up in whorls all over its body. A prize-winning Abyssinian will have 10 whorls, but cross-breeds only have two or three.

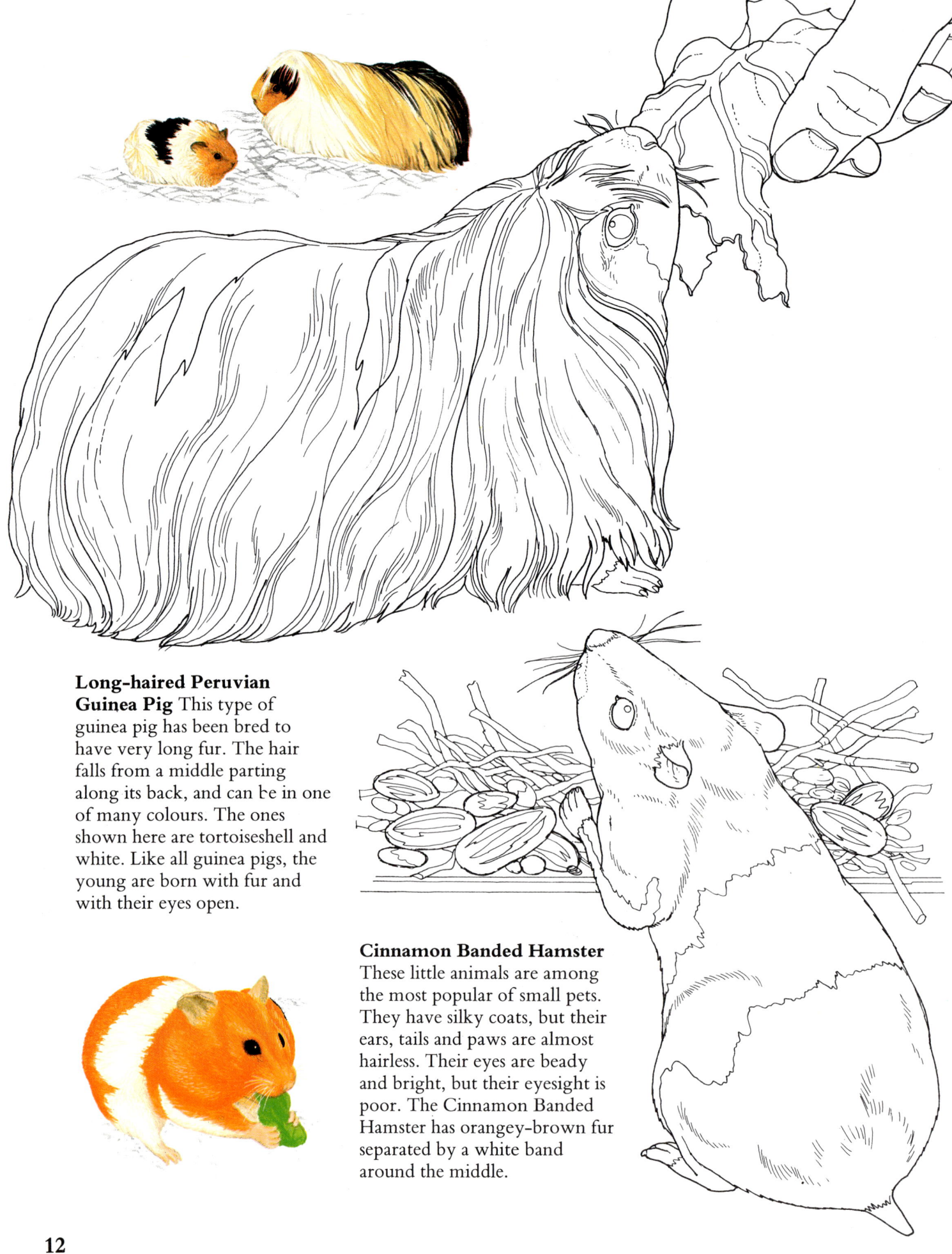

Long-haired Peruvian Guinea Pig This type of guinea pig has been bred to have very long fur. The hair falls from a middle parting along its back, and can be in one of many colours. The ones shown here are tortoiseshell and white. Like all guinea pigs, the young are born with fur and with their eyes open.

Cinnamon Banded Hamster These little animals are among the most popular of small pets. They have silky coats, but their ears, tails and paws are almost hairless. Their eyes are beady and bright, but their eyesight is poor. The Cinnamon Banded Hamster has orangey-brown fur separated by a white band around the middle.

Black-eyed Cream Hamster
This hamster has pale, biscuity-coloured fur and shiny black eyes. Here it is seen biting into a sunflower seed – a favourite hamster food. They usually store food in pouches inside their cheeks, and carry it off to a hidden food store until they are hungry.

Dutch Mice These pet mice have the 'Dutch' markings of white with patches of colour around the eyes and the back of the body. Black-and-white Dutch mice are very common. Mice should be given an exercise wheel in order to keep them healthy and trim. They also like to be given a run around outside the cage.

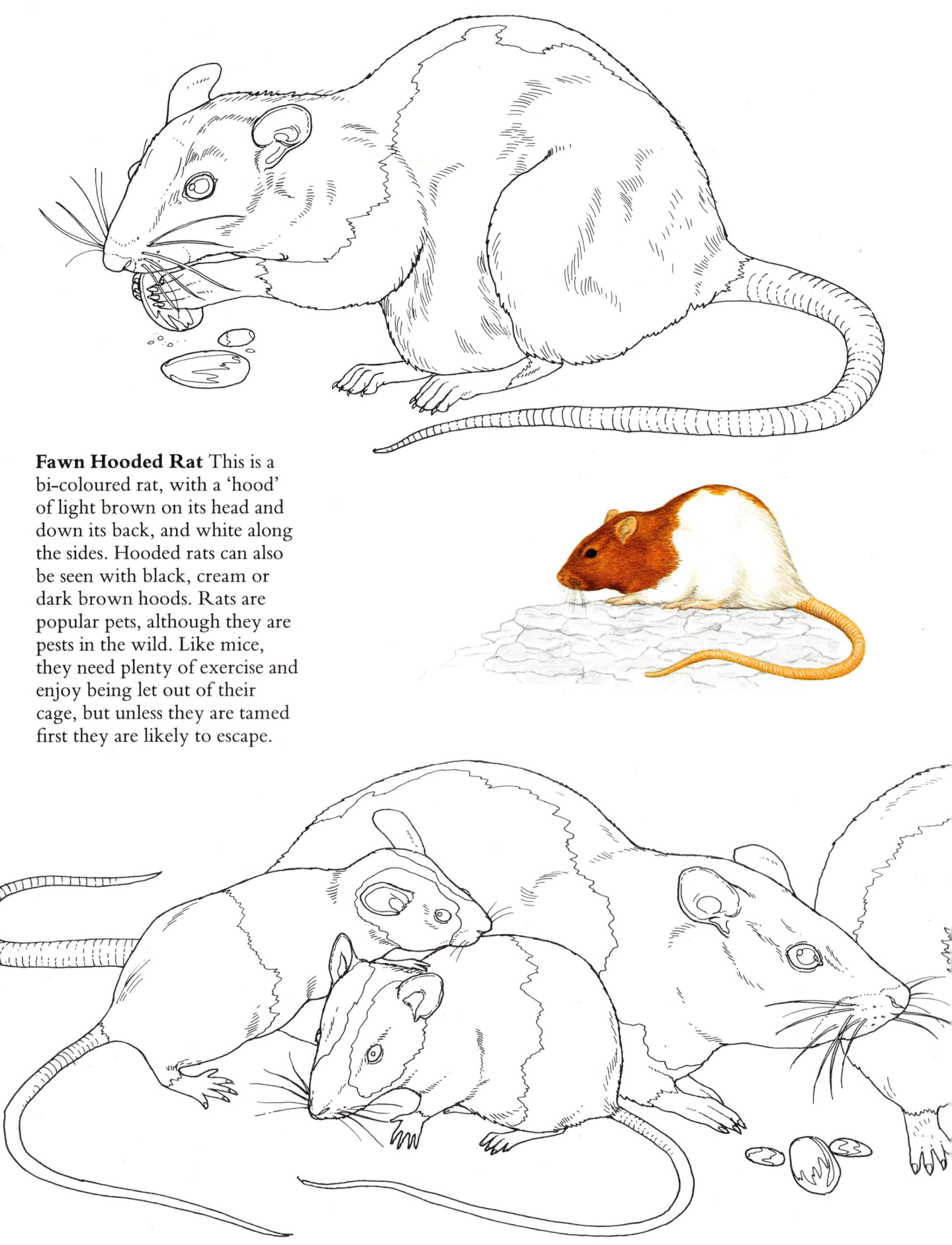

Fawn Hooded Rat This is a bi-coloured rat, with a 'hood' of light brown on its head and down its back, and white along the sides. Hooded rats can also be seen with black, cream or dark brown hoods. Rats are popular pets, although they are pests in the wild. Like mice, they need plenty of exercise and enjoy being let out of their cage, but unless they are tamed first they are likely to escape.

Tortoises and Terrapins

At one time, millions of Mediterranean tortoises were taken from their homes to other countries to be sold as pets. Many died on these journeys, and they were also in danger of dying out in their natural surroundings. Because of this, traders are no longer allowed to bring Mediterranean tortoises into Common Market countries, although other types are still sold. Terrapins are also shipped in from other countries, but many people would like to see this banned too. Both these animals are reptiles and so are cold-blooded (in other words, the warmth of their bodies depends on the warmth of their surroundings). The delicate terrapins from tropical countries are not always given the heat they need, and many die of cold. Some terrapins need the warmth of a specially heated tank, called a vivarium. They live partly on water and partly on land, and there should be some stones in the tank so that they can climb in and out of the water as they wish.

Red-eared Terrapin These terrapins from the tropical Gulf States of the USA must be kept in a heated tank, as they cannot live in our cooler climate. Even if they are kept warm, their life is likely to be shorter than it would be in their own country. They are attractive, brightly-coloured little animals, with a stripey green and yellow body, and a red spot behind the eye.

Tortoise These Mediterranean tortoises are no longer brought into Common Market countries, as they are in danger of dying out in their natural homes. The Greek tortoise (top) is brown with dark markings. The shell can be 30 centimetres long. Hermann's tortoise (bottom) is the same size as the Greek, but is often more brightly coloured.

Fish

Fish can be kept in ponds or in special tanks called aquariums. The fish that live in ponds must be able to survive normal temperature changes throughout the year, unless they are moved to a tank indoors during the winter months. The pond should be planted with water weeds, which give off the oxygen the fish need to breathe. In a well-kept pond the fish can lead a healthy, natural life, sheltering among the weeds and feeding on the tiny animal and plant life that grow there.

More delicate fish need to be kept in an aquarium. This should also be planted with weeds. If you want to keep the brightly-coloured fish that are found in tropical waters, you will have to fit a special heating device to your aquarium in order to keep it at a steady, warm temperature.

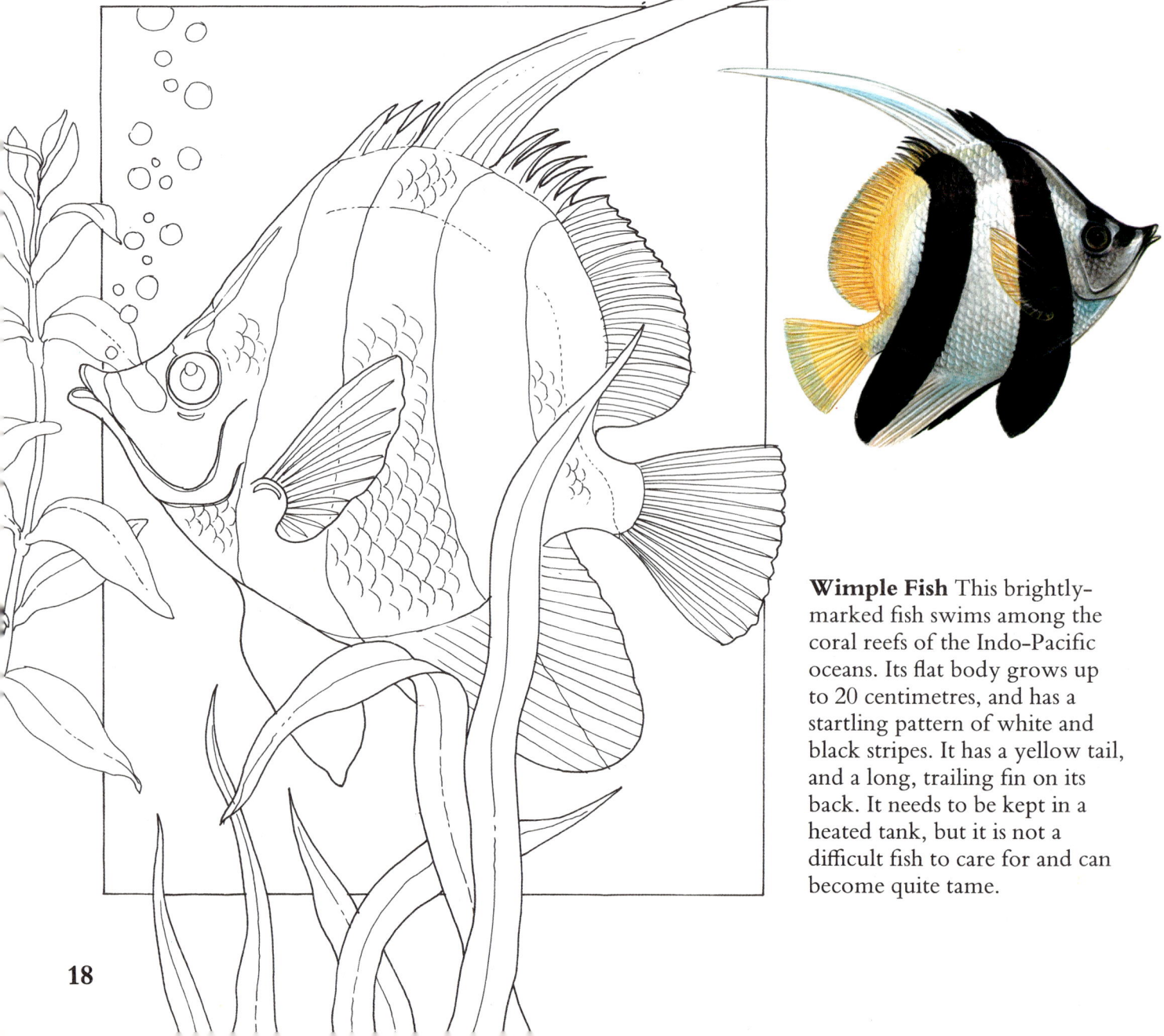

Wimple Fish This brightly-marked fish swims among the coral reefs of the Indo-Pacific oceans. Its flat body grows up to 20 centimetres, and has a startling pattern of white and black stripes. It has a yellow tail, and a long, trailing fin on its back. It needs to be kept in a heated tank, but it is not a difficult fish to care for and can become quite tame.

Common Goldfish This hardy fish is quite at home in an outdoor pond, where it can swim freely and feed on the weeds and pond life that make up its natural food. Its colour can be any shade between a pale gold and a bright red-gold although baby goldfish are always a dull green.

Shubunkins These are also a type of goldfish, but their bodies are blue with black and red markings. The London Shubunkin can live in an outdoor pond, but the long-tailed Bristol Shubunkins are better off in an aquarium.

Moorish Idol Although the Moorish Idol looks rather like the Wimple Fish, it comes from a different family. It is also much more difficult to keep, as it sometimes refuses to eat in the aquarium. The body is banded with white, black and yellow, and it has a long back fin. Young fish have spines at the corners of the mouth, and adults have horns near the eyes.

Blue Ring Angelfish This fish can grow up to 40 centimetres, and needs to be given plenty of space in the aquarium. The brown body is marked with blue lines, and a blue ring just behind the eye. The blue markings on the face fade as the fish gets older. Angelfish do not like sharing the aquarium with others of the same type, and fight if they are kept together.

Birds

Budgerigars and canaries are often kept alone, but both birds much prefer to live among their own kind. They are happiest in aviaries (large, roomy cages), where they have plenty of room to fly about. The budgerigar is a type of parrot, and the canary is a finch. The two birds should not be kept together in the same cage, as the robust budgerigar will bully the more delicate canary.

Budgerigars come from Australia, where they live in flocks in dry, desert-like areas. They fly long distances in search of water and food. The birds were first brought to Europe as pets in the last century.

Canaries first became popular in the 15th century, because of their tuneful song. In the wild, they live in flocks in the forests of the Canary Islands, Madeira and the Azores.

Roller Canary This type of canary is kept more for its attractive song than for its colouring. Some Rollers are yellow and brown, as here, but others are a dullish brown all over. A trained bird can teach another to sing, in its soft, rolling voice. Untrained Rollers also make good pets.

Light Green Budgerigar This is the natural colour of budgerigars in the wild. The head, face and wings are yellow with black markings, and the chest is green.

Cinnamon Grey Budgerigar Budgerigars have been carefully bred over the years to develop a wider variety of colours. In the Cinnamon Grey, the wing and head markings have become a soft brown. The chest is grey and the tail is mauve.

Budgerigar Colours These are some of the different colours and markings that have been developed out of the wild budgerigar. Some have no markings, such as the white Albino or the yellow Lutino. Others have a yellow or white chest to match the wings and head, and only the lower half of the body is in the usual green or blue. Whatever the colour, if the top of the beak is blue, the budgerigar is a male. If it is brown, it is a female.

Kingfisher Books, Grisewood & Dempsey Ltd,
Elsley House, 24–30 Great Titchfield Street,
London W1P 7AD.
This edition published in 1990 by Kingfisher Books.
10 9 8 7 6 5 4 3
First published in 1987 under the Piccolo imprint by
Pan Books Ltd.
© Grisewood & Dempsey Ltd, 1987
All rights reserved.
ISBN 0 86272 591 7
Text written by: Meg Sanders
Editor: Deri Robins
Designer: Ben White
Illustrated by: Hayward Artists
Phototypeset by SPAN, Lingfield, Surrey
Printed in Spain